From Caterpillar to Butterfly
Notes and activities by Karina Law, author and educational consultant

Each book in the *Lifecycles* series traces a story of growth and change.
Here are some ideas of how to get the most of *From Caterpillar to Butterfly*:

Responding to the text
Once you have read through the book with children, ask open-ended questions to assess their comprehension.
- Can they think of other animals that shed their skin, for example, a snake?
- What dangers does the caterpillar need to protect itself from? How does it do this?
- What happens after the pupa splits open?
- What happens to butterflies during the winter months?

Features of non-fiction texts
Challenge children to locate specific information in the book using the contents page (page 6) or the index (page 29). Where would they look to find out about hibernation? Where would they look to find out what caterpillars eat? Which page would they turn to if they wanted to read about the caterpillar's enemies?

Look at the glossary of butterfly words on page 28. How many of these words were the children already familiar with? Which words are new to them? Why are the words in alphabetical order?

Language and literacy
Look for poems, rhymes and stories about butterflies or caterpillars to share with the children. For example, *The Very Hungry Caterpillar*, by Eric Carle.

'Lifecycles' is a frequently studied topic with many cross-curricular links. Children can use *From Caterpillar to Butterfly* as a starting point for studying changes that other animals go through. Collect pictures of animals at different stages. For example, compare a cygnet with an adult swan; a tadpole with a frog.

These are some suggestions for continuing the learning process through practical, fun activities.

Lifecycle cards

This activity will help to reinforce children's understanding of the lifecycle of a butterfly.

You will need four blank pieces of card for each child (pre-cut to A2 size), a pencil, crayons or felt-tip pens.

What to do:
1. Give each child four blank cards.

2. Talk to the children about the lifecycle of a butterfly and ask them to draw a picture on each card representing each of the four main stages: egg, caterpillar, pupa, adult butterfly. Help them to label their pictures.

3. Jumble up the cards and ask the children to organize them into the correct sequence. Encourage them to tell you about each stage as they do so.

Butterfly painting

Make this butterfly painting and then ask the children to find other symmetrical things in the world around them.

You will need a large sheet of thick paper, a paint brush, poster paints

What to do:
1. Fold the large sheet of paper in half.

2. Open the paper out and paint one half of a butterfly on one side of the crease. Talk about the different features of the butterfly, including the head, wings and antennae.

3. Fold the other side of the paper down over the painted side and smooth the paper down to help the paint stick.

4. Open the sheet of paper out again to reveal a whole, symmetrical butterfly.

5. Once the painting is dry, help the children to label the different parts of the butterfly.

This edition published in 2014

Editor: April McCroskie
Language Consultant: Professor Viv Edwards

Dr Gerald Legg holds a doctorate in zoology from
Manchester University. He is the Keeper of the
Booth Museum of Natural History in Brighton.

Carolyn Scrace is a graduate of Brighton College
of Art, specialising in design and illustration. She has
worked in animation, advertising and children's
fiction. She is a major contributor to the popular
Worldwise series.

Professor Viv Edwards is professor of Language
in Education and director of the National Centre for
Language and Literacy at the University
of Reading.

David Salariya was born in Dundee, Scotland,
where he studied illustration and printmaking,
specialising in book design in his postgraduate year,
he has designed and created many new series of
children's books for publishers in the UK and overseas.

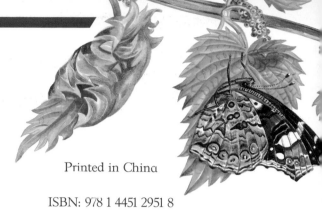

Printed in China

ISBN: 978 1 4451 2951 8
Dewey classification 595.78

First published in the UK by
Franklin Watts
338 Euston Road, London, NW1 3BH

Franklin Watts Australia
Level 17/207 Kent Street, Sydney, NSW 2000

Franklin Watts is a division of Hachette Children's Books,
an Hachette UK company
www.hachette.co.uk

An SBC Book conceived, edited and designed by
The Salariya Book Company
25 Marlborough Place Brighton BN1 1UB

A CIP catalogue record for this book is available from
the British Library

lifecycles

From Caterpillar
to Butterfly

Written by Dr Gerald Legg
Illustrated by Carolyn Scrace

Created & Designed by David Salariya

W
FRANKLIN WATTS
LONDON • SYDNEY

A butterfly starts life as an egg. A caterpillar hatches from the egg. The caterpillar grows and changes into a pupa. A beautiful butterfly hatches from the pupa. In this book you can see this amazing life cycle unfold.

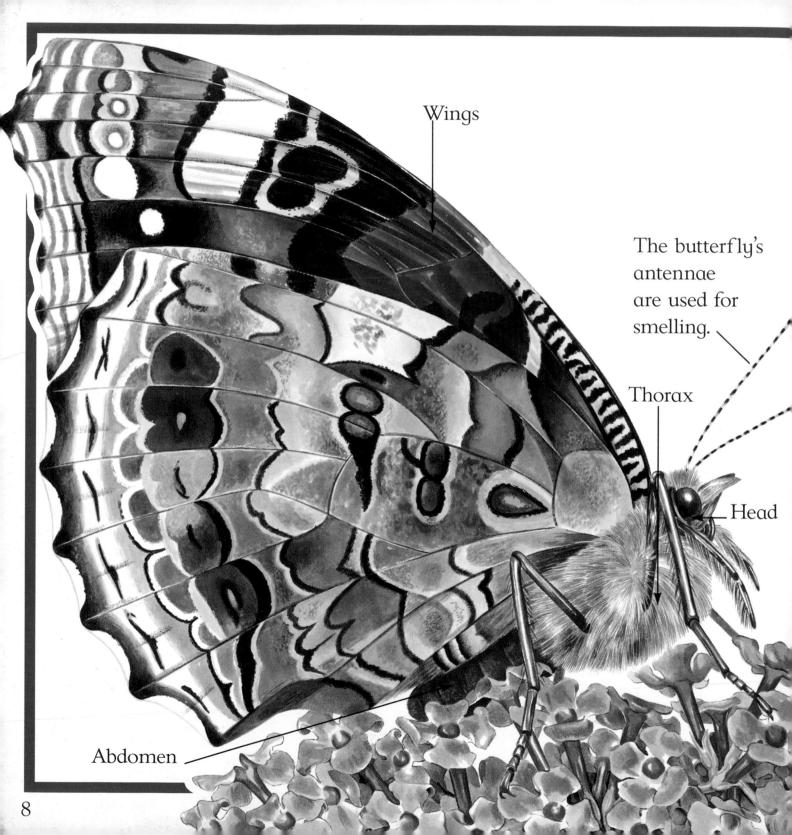

Wings

The butterfly's antennae are used for smelling.

Thorax

Head

Abdomen

8

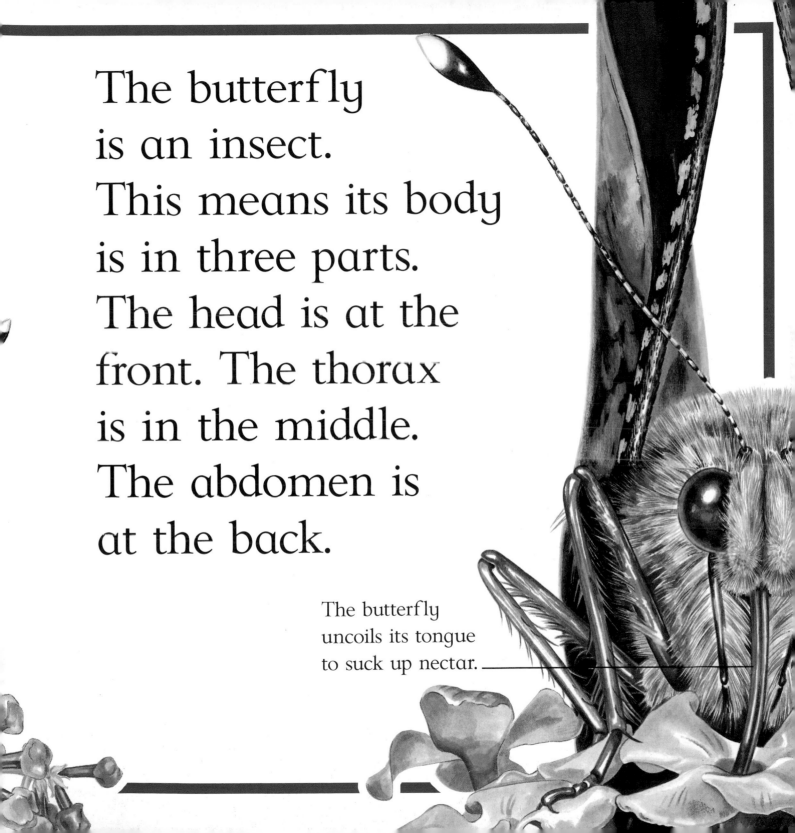

The butterfly
is an insect.
This means its body
is in three parts.
The head is at the
front. The thorax
is in the middle.
The abdomen is
at the back.

The butterfly
uncoils its tongue
to suck up nectar.

Female butterflies
lay their eggs on leaves.
The eggs stick to the leaves
so they will not fall off.
The baby insect grows
inside the sticky egg.
When it hatches
it is a caterpillar.

Leaf

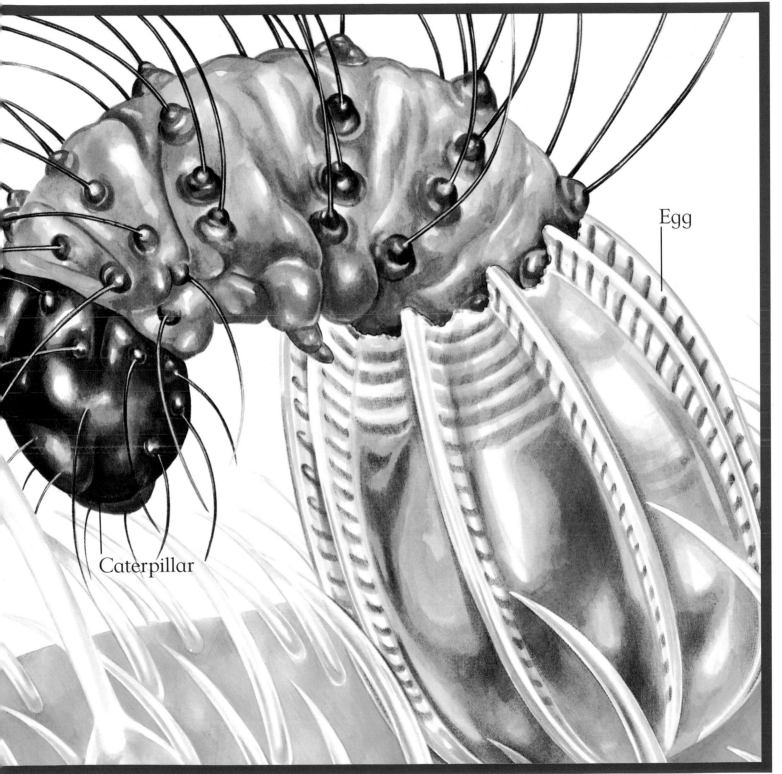

Egg

Caterpillar

11

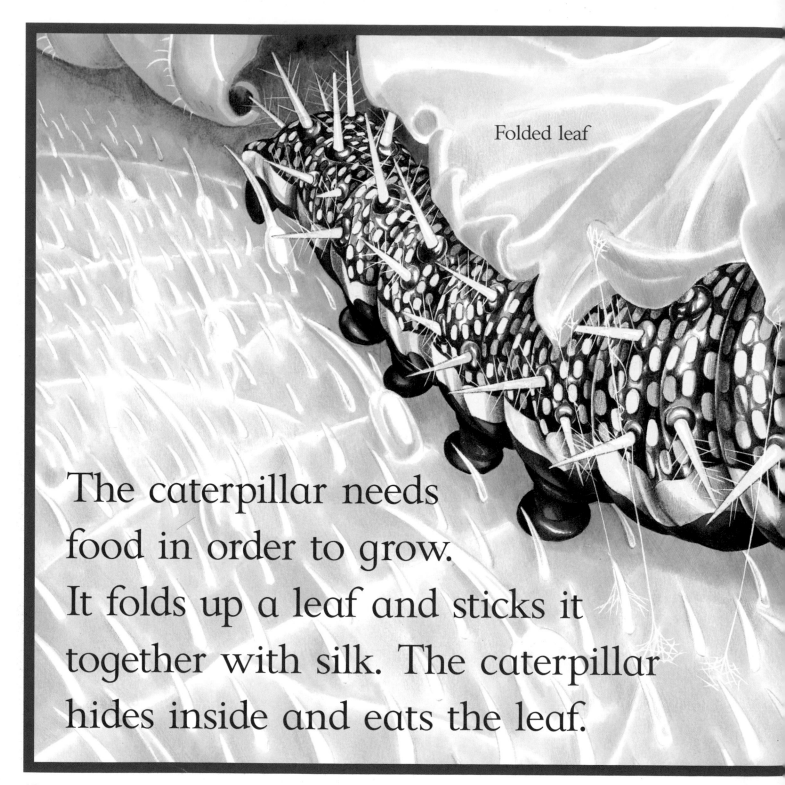

Folded leaf

The caterpillar needs
food in order to grow.
It folds up a leaf and sticks it
together with silk. The caterpillar
hides inside and eats the leaf.

Silk ———

Mouth

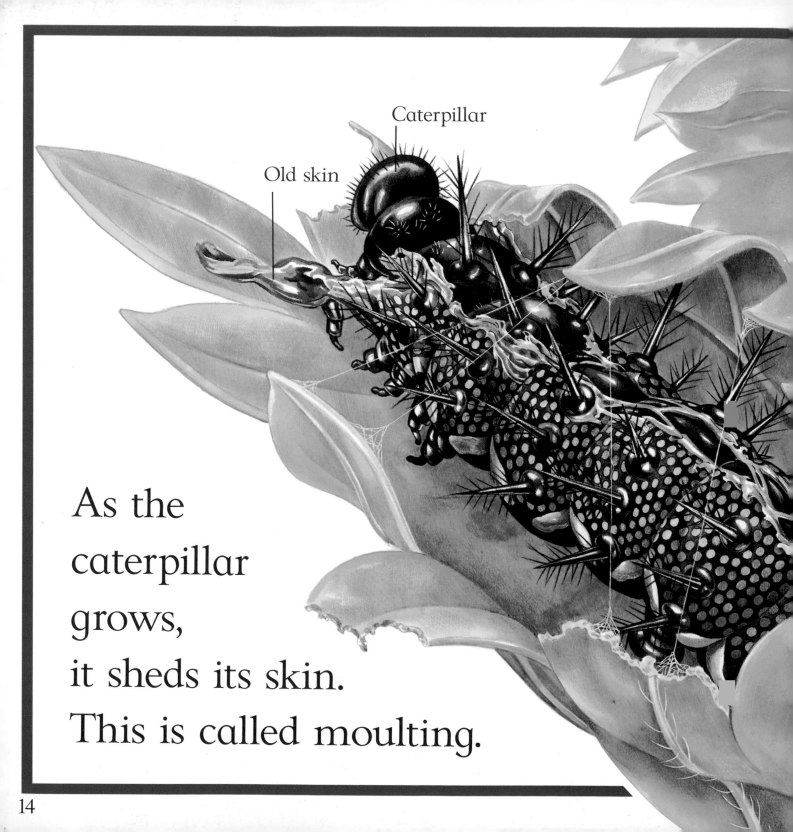

Caterpillar

Old skin

As the
caterpillar
grows,
it sheds its skin.
This is called moulting.

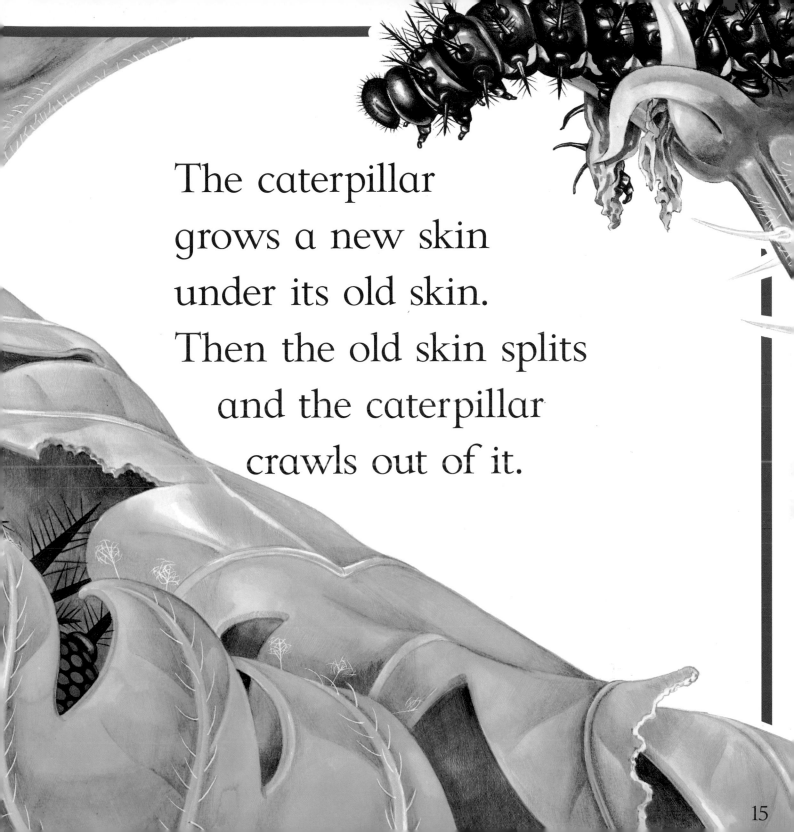

The caterpillar
grows a new skin
under its old skin.
Then the old skin splits
and the caterpillar
crawls out of it.

Bird

Many animals like
to eat caterpillars.
They make a juicy treat
for spiders, wasps
and birds.

Spider

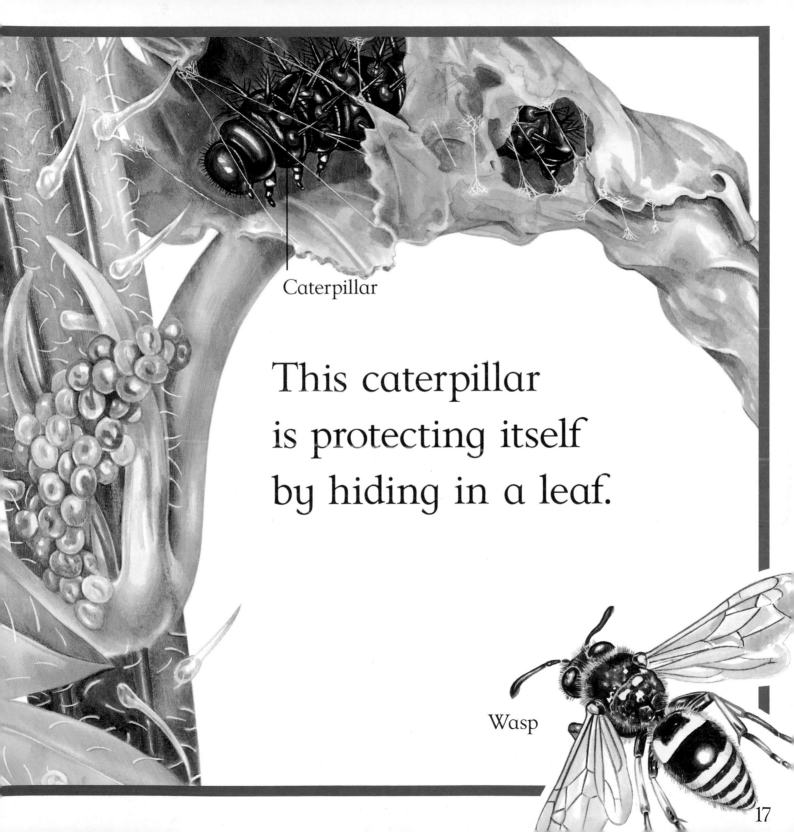

Caterpillar

This caterpillar
is protecting itself
by hiding in a leaf.

Wasp

17

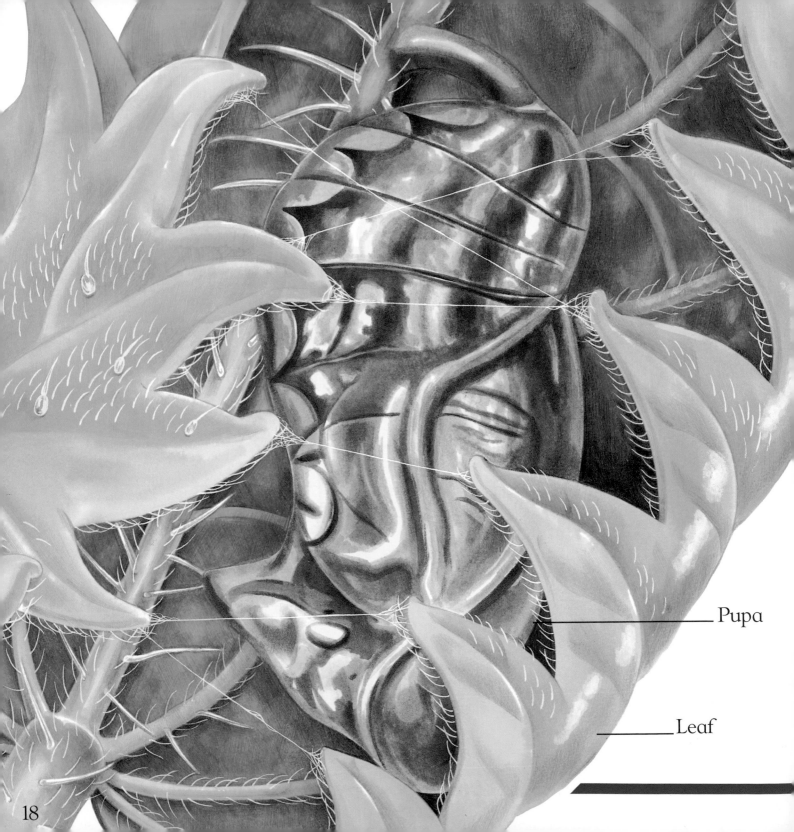

Pupa

Leaf

18

The fully grown caterpillar on a leaf stem.

The caterpillar hangs by a silk thread.

The caterpillar changes into a pupa.

It takes a few hours for the pupa to form.

The butterfly grows inside the pupa.

When the caterpillar is fully grown, it gets ready to turn into a butterfly. It hangs down on a silk thread from a leaf stem. Then it sheds its skin for the last time to form a pupa. Inside the pupa, the caterpillar changes into a butterfly.

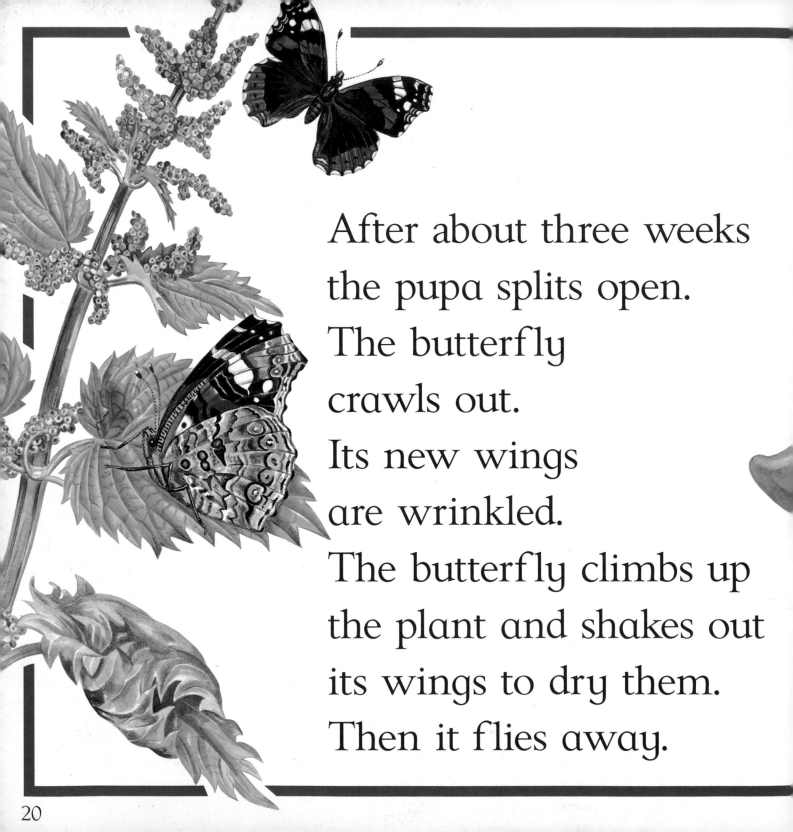

After about three weeks
the pupa splits open.
The butterfly
crawls out.
Its new wings
are wrinkled.
The butterfly climbs up
the plant and shakes out
its wings to dry them.
Then it flies away.

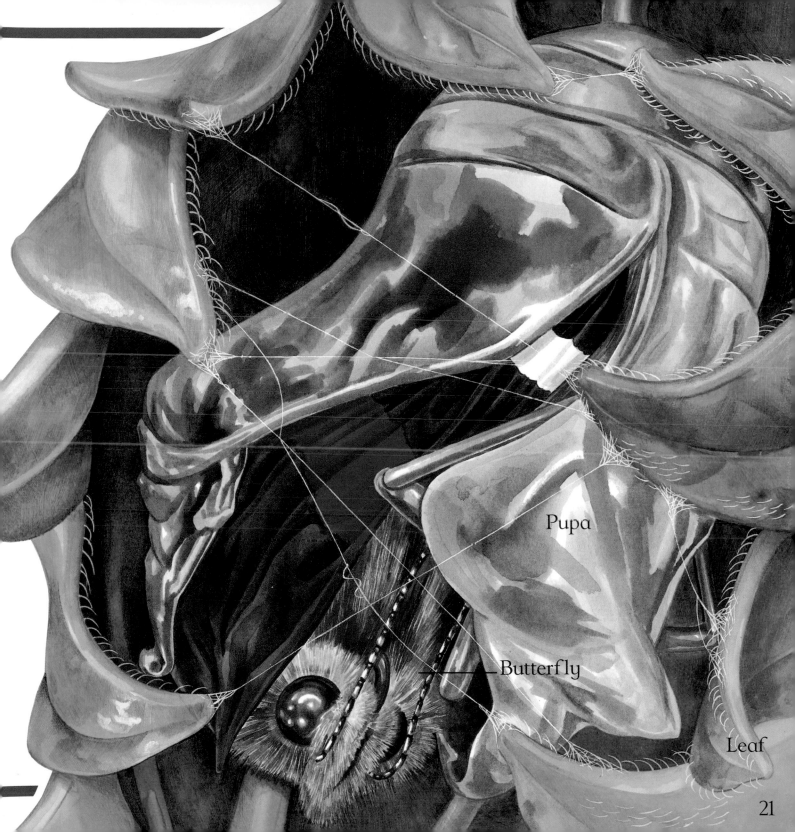

Pupa

Butterfly

Leaf

Male and female butterflies visit the same flowers to feed. Sometimes, they rest on a leaf to mate. The female butterfly then flies away to lay her eggs.

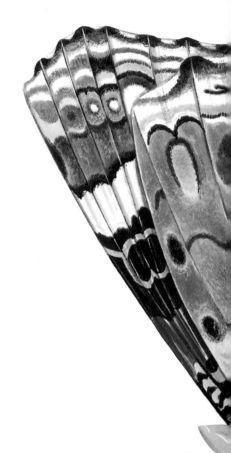

Leaf

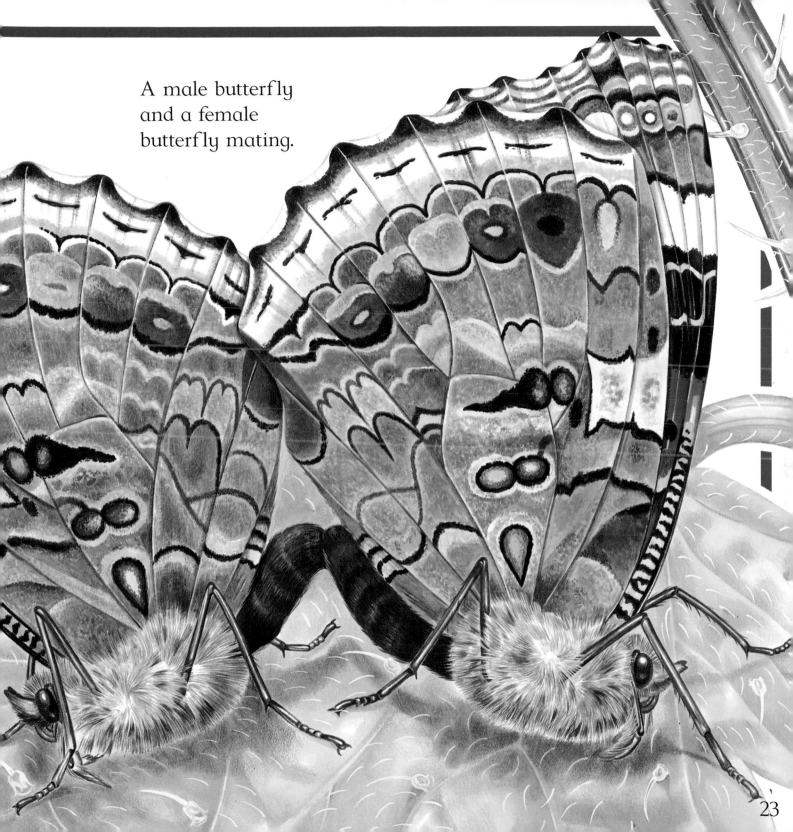

A male butterfly and a female butterfly mating.

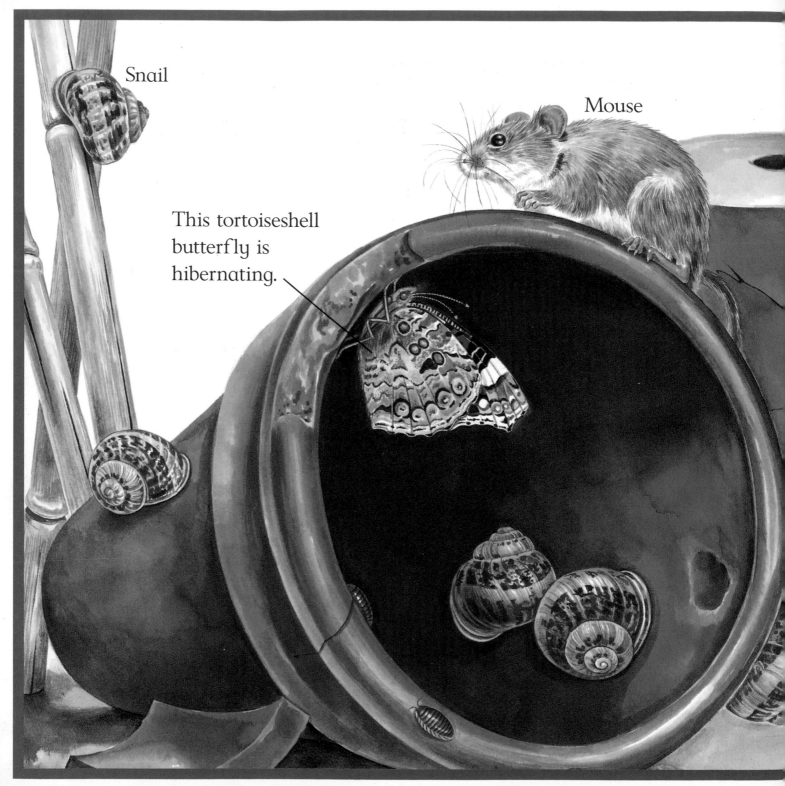

Snail

Mouse

This tortoiseshell
butterfly is
hibernating.

24

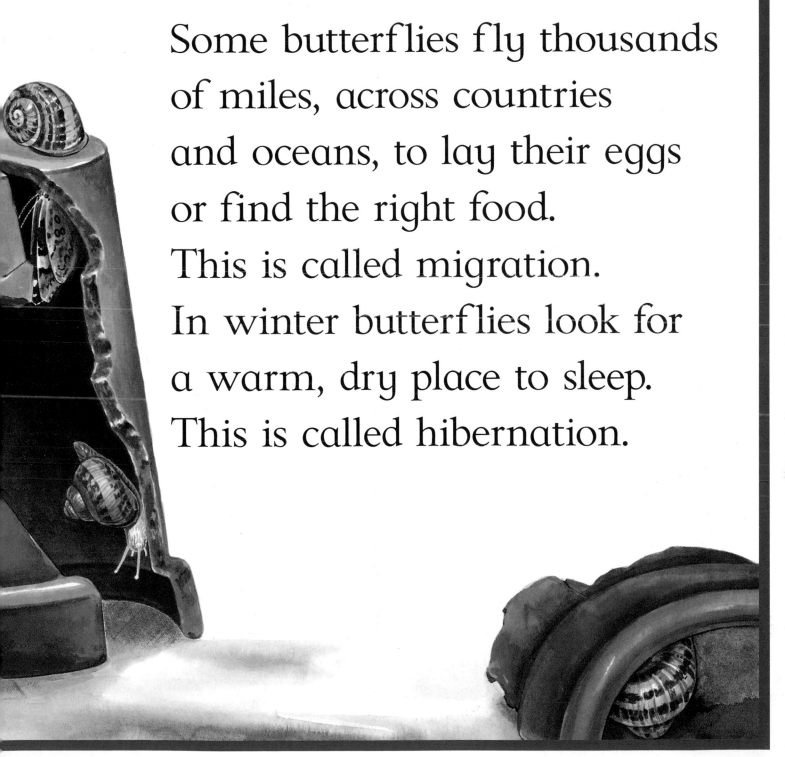

Some butterflies fly thousands
of miles, across countries
and oceans, to lay their eggs
or find the right food.
This is called migration.
In winter butterflies look for
a warm, dry place to sleep.
This is called hibernation.

Butterfly facts

A butterfly is an insect that flies during the day. It has antennae with club-shaped tips.

A moth is an insect that flies mainly at night. It has antennae that are thread-like or feathery.

The largest butterfly is the birdwing butterfly of New Guinea. It is 28 centimetres long.

The smallest butterfly is the dwarf blue butterfly of South Africa. It is just over 1 centimetre long.

The best flyer is the painted lady butterfly, which is found in most countries of the world. It can fly 1,000 kilometres without resting.

The fastest flyer is the monarch butterfly of North America. It can fly at 32 kilometres an hour.

Monarch butterflies hibernate in groups of tens of thousands.

Butterflies beat their wings between 8 and 12 times a second.

Some butterflies only live for one day, but other butterflies can live for 4-5 months.

The owl butterfly of South America has markings on its wings that make it look like an owl. This helps to frighten its enemies.

The caterpillar of the Jamaican swallow-tail butterfly hides by pretending to be a bird dropping. This way its enemies do not recognise that it is a tasty meal.

Zebra butterflies from the Americas are brightly coloured. They do not bother to hide since they are poisonous and are left alone by their enemies.

The African leaf butterfly lies down among dead leaves to rest. Its wings look exactly like dead leaves, so its enemies do not see it.

The sixty-nine butterfly of South America looks like it has the number 69 on its wings.

Egg

Developing caterpillar

Pupa

Adult butterfly

The growth of a butterfly

In the pictures above you can see how a butterfly grows from a tiny egg to a caterpillar then into a pupa and finally into a magnificent butterfly.

Butterfly words

Abdomen
The rear part of an insect's body.

Antennae
The feelers on the head of an insect. Antennae are used for smelling.

Caterpillar
The stage in the life of a butterfly or moth just after it hatches from the egg.

Hibernation
When an animal sleeps through the winter.

Insect
An animal with a hard outer skin. An insect's body has 3 parts: a head, a thorax and an abdomen. Insects have 6 legs and 2 antennae.

Mating
The joining of a male (father) and a female (mother) to make babies.

Migration
When an animal travels a long way, at certain times of the year, to find a better place to live.

Moulting
When an animal sheds its skin in order to grow.

Nectar
Sweet, sugary syrup made by flowers to attract insects.

Pupa
The stage in the life of a butterfly or moth between the caterpillar and the adult insect.

Thorax
The middle part of an insect's body.

Index

A
abdomen 8, 9, 28
antennae 8, 26, 28

B
birds 16
body 9
butterfly 7, 8, 9, 10, 19, 20, 21, 24, 25, 26, 27, 28

C
caterpillar 7, 10, 11, 12, 14, 15, 16, 17, 19, 27, 28

E
egg 7, 10, 11, 22, 28

F
flowers 22, 28

H
head 8, 9
hibernation 24, 25, 26, 28

I
insect 9, 10, 26, 28

L
leaf 10, 12, 17, 18, 19, 22, 27

M
mating 22, 23, 28
migration 25, 28
moths 26, 28
moulting 14, 28

N
nectar 9, 28

P
pupa 7, 18, 19, 20, 21, 28

S
silk 12, 13, 19
skin 14, 15, 19, 28
spiders 16

T
thorax 8, 9, 28
tongue 9

W
wasps 16, 17
wings 8, 20, 26, 27

29